WORKBOOK

for

DARE TO LEAD

*Brave Work, Tough Conversations,
Whole Hearts By Brené Brown*

The Review Press

Contents

INTRODUCTION 1

PART ONE: RUMBLING WITH VULNERABILTY 3

Section One: The Moment and the Myths 3

KEY TAKEAWAYS 5

SELF EXAMINATIONS 9

CHECKLIST 14

SECTION 2: THE CALL TO COURAGE 18

KEY TAKEAWAYS 19

SELF EXAMINATIONS 22

CHECKLIST 28

SECTION THREE: THE ARMORY 32

KEY TAKEAWAYS 32

SELF EXAMINATIONS 35

CHECKLISTS 41

SECTION FOUR: SHAME AND EMPATHY 44

KEY TAKEAWAYS 45

SELF EXAMINTIONS 47

CHECKLISTS 53

SECTION FIVE: CURIOSITY AND GROUNDED
CONFIDENCE..56
    KEY TAKEAWAYS 57
    SELF EXAMINATIONS 60
    CHECKLISTS..65

PART TWO: LIVING INTO OUR VALUES 68
    KEY TAKEAWAYS 69
    SELF EXAMINATIONS 72
    CHECKLISTS..78

PART THREE: BRAVING TRUST...................................81
    KEY TAKEAWAYS 82
    SELF EXAMINATIONS 85
    CHECKLISTS...91

PART FOUR: LEARNING TO RISE 94
    KEY TAKEAWAYS 94
    SELF EXAMINATIONS 97
    CHECKLISTS..103

INTRODUCTION

Brené Brown's dare to lead is a leadership book that deviates from the norm of leadership. The book is a result of the author's two decades of research and experiences inside a lot of organizations to make leaders better in their jobs especially in this new age. The book focuses more on easily forgotten emotions like being courageous, bravery, vulnerability, shame, confidence, trust, etc. which are properly discussed for the readers to digest throughout the four parts of the book.

One of the major things that will be discussed in the book is how to be a brave and daring leader. Being daring means being courageous, vulnerable and trustworthy, and being able to communicate these emotions with your team members.

Contrary to what people think, courage is not a personal or behavioral trait. It is a skill just like communication that should be learned, and properly applied by a leader the same goes for the other emotions. At the heart of daring leadership is a deeply human truth that is rarely acknowledged which is mostly courage and fear which unfortunately pops up at the same time.

The book encourages leaders in every sphere of life to rumble with vulnerability to get courageous, be self-aware, and practice self-love, and to cultivate a work environment where brave work, tough conversations and whole hearts are necessary.

PART ONE: RUMBLING WITH VULNERABILTY

Section One: The Moment and the Myths

This section highlighted how people are advised to think in certain ways about certain things.

The author talks about the three lessons she learned from the Roosevelt quote which are the physics of vulnerability: this talks about how possible it is that we might often face challenges or take risks but still not succeed. As the term daring is acknowledging the fact that you might fail at what you are about to do but still give it a go. Many successful people have at some point failed or been disappointed or heartbroken but still kept going and that's why we know of them today.

The second lesson is learning about vulnerability as the emotion that we experience during times of uncertainty, risk, and emotional exposure. It is the courage to face situations when you have no idea what comes next. After a number of interviews the term vulnerability still emerges with one major meaning that is the ability to show strength even in times where you are supposed to show weakness, no one defines vulnerability as defeat.

Vulnerable experiences are not easy; they can definitely make us uneasy and always overprotective. For someone to have the strength and grace to show up while facing all these experiences with a whole heart and no assurances the person is said to be very courageous.

The third lesson is that if you don't try and take risks you won't develop or grow. There are a lot of people in the world today who are not courageous and will spend all their time and energy advising you and judging you when you do try to be courageous and take risks all they ever do is criticize and make you scared. We are advised to know better than to take the advice of

0

0

5

anybody who has not taken the kind of risks you are about to take, no matter how correct they might seem. We should however pay more attention to people who come from where we are. We cannot be as brave as we want to be if we allow people's ideas of us to be what we think of ourselves.

The author also talks about how we should not allow ourselves to be consumed by myths, like vulnerability is a weakness or thoughts such as, I cannot be vulnerable or I can control how vulnerable I can be. This kind of thinking allows you to become even more vulnerable than you can.

KEY TAKEAWAYS

1. To be vulnerable is to be brave enough to know that failure is inevitable, but still going through it.

2. Being vulnerable does not in any way mean you are weak and being vulnerable is

definitely not an easy experience to anyone.

3. You need to have experienced failure and vulnerability for you to understand the fears of others and what they are going through in moments of failures.

4. Try often to find a balance between the opinions of what people think about you and caring about what they think.

5. People often commit the fallacy of assuming that vulnerability is equal to weakness. Being vulnerable is the emotion we experience during time of pure risk and it equals to being courageous.

6. Always choose to own your vulnerability so that you understand in what manner to rumble with the emotions and stay aligned with your core values.

7. Denying vulnerability means ultimately letting fear drive your behavior and actions.

8. Wisdom and experience validates the importance of being vulnerable and accepting it for personal growth.

9. Research shows that we do not derive strength from individualism but rather from our collective ability to communicate and work together.

10. It is mostly difficult to assume the critical role vulnerability plays in leadership especially when it is equated with loopholes, liability and in extreme situations, death.

11. Do not try to ship off uncertainty, risk and emotional exposure in a bid to deny vulnerability. It only bankrupts courage by definition.

12. Contrary to what people think, we need trust to be vulnerable and we need to be vulnerable in order to build trust. They both go hand in hand and they involve taking risk, to betray one is to destroy both.

13. Trust is earned in the simplest ways like remembering little details and not through heroic deeds.

14. Vulnerability is very hard to practice but it brings out the magic and creativity in everyone. It is also the core of all emotions and the birthplace of joy, love and belonging.

15. Psychological safety is very important especially when working in teams because it gives a free environment where people learn and respect each other and also where a sense of confidence is built around all members.

SELF EXAMINATIONS

1. What does vulnerability mean to you?

_____

_____

_____

_____

_____

2. In what way have you shown vulnerability in whatever you are doing?

_____

_____

_____

_____

_____

3. How have you shown bravery as a leader?

_____

_____

_____

_____

_____

4. How often have you faced disappointments?

_____

_____

_____

_____

_____

5. Mention the moments when you have felt vulnerable to a situation or person?

_____

_____

_____

_____

_____

6. What does living an armor-free life mean to you?

_____

_____

_____

_____

_____

7. Who are the people whose feedback is important to you?

_____

_____

_____

_____

_____

8. How often do you allow the opinions of others define you?

_____

_____

_____

_____

_____

9. How does being courageous go with being vulnerable?

_____

_____

_____

_____

_____

10.   What outcome have you had when you allowed fear drive your emotions?

_____

_____

_____

_____

11. What is your opinion on independence and not sowing your vulnerability?

_____

_____

_____

_____

12. In what situation have you ever chosen to be vulnerable when there is a lot at stake?

_____

_____

_____

_____

_____

13. How has your vulnerability led to betrayal by someone or your feelings?

_____

_____

_____

_____

_____

14. In what way have you faked vulnerability in order to keep a safety net and protect yourself?

_____

_____

_____

_____

_____

15. How did you manage telling half-truths to avoid difficult conversations and situations?

_____

_____

_____

_____

_____

CHECKLIST

1. Do you accept vulnerability?

Yes [   ]   No [   ]

2. Do you consider yourself as someone who is brave?

Yes [   ]   No [   ]

3. Have you ever been disappointed or faced with failure?

Yes [ ]   No [ ]

4. Knowing well that you cannot control the outcome of a situation, would you still go through with it?

Yes [ ]   No [ ]

5. Do you believe that being vulnerable means being weak?

Yes [ ]   No [ ]

6. Do you embrace uncertainties and failures by living armor-free?

Yes [ ]   No [ ]

7. Do you have people who love and care for you because of your imperfections and not despite them?

Yes [ ]   No [ ]

8. Does courage align with vulnerable?

Yes [ ]   No [ ]

9. Do you let fear drive your thinking and behavior?

Yes [ ]   No [ ]

10.   Do you need anyone to survive?

Yes [ ]   No [ ]

11. Would you choose to be vulnerable in a situation where you are risking everything you worked for?

Yes [ ]   No [ ]

12. Do you think vulnerability and trust has a strong connection?

Yes [ ]   No [ ]

13. Do you feel safe taking risks and being vulnerable in front of your team?

Yes [ ]   No [ ]

14.Do you practice fake vulnerability to your team in order to create a safety net?

Yes [ ]   No [ ]

15.Do you have a psychologically safe environment with people in your life?

Yes [ ]   No [ ]

SECTION 2: THE CALL TO COURAGE

Many of us get that thinking, what now feeling when we no longer know how to drive forward. This may sometimes lead us to unrealistic schedules or goals that when we cannot meet up with, will keep us in constant chaos.

When we are clear, we are kind. Most times, we avoid telling the truth, because we feel like that's the best thing to do. People need to hear the truth even if they seem like they would not be able to handle it you might come off as rude or unsupportive but in reality you are being fair. If we want to ensure the development or growth of our friends we should be able to risk uncomfortable situations and tell them the truth at all times.

The author also talks about self doubt which is the reason why we are always overprotective or why we always think we are not enough. And also the reason why we find it difficult to share our feelings with others which are fear of what they might think of us or we think of how no one else around us is honest, so why do we have to be.

We are encouraged to leading or living our lives from fear and strive to be courageous and faithful.

KEY TAKEAWAYS

1. People often prefer to be unclear about emotions in order to appear kind but in reality, it is unkind and unfair to leave people with unclear thoughts.

2. When in fear, it is easier to take the pattern of assuming we are not enough, shying away from honesty, blaming others for your shortcomings and assuming superiority over the situation.

3. As leaders, fear is a constant emotion and it is more evident when you don't want to share that you have made bad decisions that would affect everyone.

4. Finding the right medium of communication when dealing with your team is most effective and often leads to desired results.

5. Even with the wealth of knowledge and experience, it is important to have an open environment where your team is free to

pitch their ideas and minimize the band wagon effect.

6. It is not okay to just be a realist or just be a realist or just be the reality checker, it is important to be both realistic and optimistic.

7. In as much as optimism is laudable, it is also necessary to possess the discipline to confront your current reality.

8. Apologizing as leaders is generally considered to be a sign of weakness but it actually helps to make amends with your team and spur on brave leadership.

9. Getting the right language and tone to communicate your vulnerability and also ask your team to have the courage to show vulnerability is very important.

10. In facing your fears as a leader, you build the courage, power and wisdom to serve others.

11. Being brave enough to be in an uncomfortable situation with your team

members is one that determines a true leader.

12.Being connected and being a part of an inclusive group sometimes is the link between productivity and work.

13.Starting the conversation on something as uncomfortable as vulnerability gives your team the feeling that it is safe to be vulnerable. This becomes their safe space.

14.When discussing vulnerability, shy away from sterile and unclear words. At that moment, your team needs to be reached at a deeper level and sterile words would not fit into that situation.

15.It is important to invest time attending to the fears and feelings of team members or suffer future time trying to manage unproductive behavior.

SELF EXAMINATIONS

1. In what way have you been unclear about your intentions in order to be kind and uncouth?

_____

_____

_____

_____

_____

2. What is the amor you put on when faced with a difficult situation?

_____

_____

_____

_____

_____

3. What are the values you apply when faced with fear especially regarding leadership?

_____

_____

_____

_____

_____

4. In what way have your anxiety and fear affected your decisions and expectations of your team?

_____

_____

_____

_____

5. How have you effectively controlled the band wagon effect in your team?

_____

_____

_____

_____

_____

6. How do you create space within your team to understand different perspectives and learning from everyone?

_____

_____

_____

_____

_____

7. How do you manage being optimistic and also being realistic?

_____

_____

_____

_____

_____

8. How do you apologize to your team and do you back it with a behavioral change?

_____

_____

_____

_____

_____

9. What language (tone) would you relate vulnerability to your subordinates?

_____

_____

_____

_____

_____

10. In what way have courage overtaken comfort when you want to get better results in serving your team?

_____

_____

_____

_____

_____

11. How connected are your team members to one another?

_____

_____

_____

_____

_____

12. Within a team, who should show initial vulnerability and why?

_____

_____

_____

_____

_____

13. What words or phrases would you use when dealing with the topic of vulnerability with your team?

_____

_____

_____

_____

_____

14. What are the communication skills you adopt when dealing with your team members?

_____

_____

_____

_____

_____

_____

15. How would you allow your team members take responsibility for their emotions so that they can put in more productive work?

_____

_____

_____

_____

_____

_____

CHECKLIST

1. Do you think being unclear about something is actually being kind especially because of the effect it might have?

Yes [ ] No [ ]

2. Do you lead with fear of the unknown?

Yes [ ]   No [ ]

3. Do you allow anxiety drive your decisions as a leader?

        Yes [   ]   No [   ]

4. Do you give a free environment for clarity by your team members?

        Yes [   ]   No [   ]

5. Are your team members effectively involved in the planning process of activities by contributing their ideas and opinions?

        Yes [   ]   No [   ]

6. Do you blindly follow optimism despite the glaring reality?

        Yes [   ]   No [   ]

7. Have you ever apologized to your team for an error of judgment or lack of clarity on a matter?

        Yes [   ]   No [   ]

8. Do you let your team members show vulnerability to you?

Yes [ ]   No [ ]

9. Does loneliness affect work and outcome of team members?

Yes [ ]   No [ ]

10. Do you choose courage over comfort in order to serve others?

Yes [ ]   No [ ]

11. Your team members have a link between each other to help ease the stress of work on them?

Yes [ ]   No [ ]

12. Do you believe that it is in first being vulnerable to your team that brings their own vulnerability?

Yes [ ]   No [ ]

13. Do you discuss feelings and emotions with your team?

Yes [ ]   No [ ]

14. Do you listen when a team member speaks about an uncomfortable personal problem?

Yes [   ]   No [   ]

15. Can leaders serve people and also try to control their feelings?

Yes [   ]   No [   ]

SECTION THREE: THE ARMORY

In this section, the author talks about the barriers of success, talks about how most times during your struggle after some time it starts to look like you are starting to progress a bit but almost immediately more and more problems emerge sometimes even worse than before but with grace intelligence and courage you later find dealing with these problems even easier.

We might try to protect ourselves with different tactics and schemes but we are still in love and we want to be loved.

KEY TAKEAWAYS

1. Wholeheartedness is going through our lives knowing that we are worthy and believe it.

2. No matter the security that people seek, it is important that we put down the armor we put up and try to integrate with the team.

3. Most companies still believe that if you share emotions from work, productivity

would be high and easier to manage. But it only enables people to build armors at work.

4. Organizations that prefer perfectionism and fall compartmentalizing of the lives of their staff always avoid vulnerability and value all-knowing over always learning which is not good for productivity.

5. When we imprison the heart, courage dies. Therefore emotions are important especially in the workplace as it always keeps us innovative and creative.

6. When we try to deny our emotions, we lose control of our physical feelings emotions drive our decision making totally without our consent.

7. Ego is the ultimate enemy of vulnerability. It encourages us to avoid the discomfort associated with feeling vulnerable or even curiosity because of its risk.

8. It is important that we recognize that everyone is different, eccentric and somewhat strange but they are to add the

small pieces of themselves to make the puzzle whole. Fitting in is not necessary and not right.

9. An armored type of leadership is constricting and also dehumanizes work. An armored leadership is just like using machines to do the work.
10. Whenever you let perfectionism drive you, shame is inevitable. It is also worthy to note that perfection is not excellence, it is not self-improvement and it is not an indicator of success.

11. Joy is the most vulnerable emotion we feel, it is fragile, beautiful and perfect all wrapped up together and when we cannot tolerate that kind of vulnerability, we move immediately to self-protection.

12. Everyone at different point of their lives have experienced pain, suffering, and the cost of it. Then we go ahead to numb that pain at the workplace to help us not to deal with it and interfere with our work. The only way we could cure numbing is by finding real comfort and a renew our spirit.

13. Life is not just full of opposites like or be killed, succeed or lose. All those are false and it just keeps us surviving instead of living.

14. People who think they are always right are actually just being unnecessarily defensive it leads to bad decisions, distrust for other people and unproductive conflict.

15. As a daring leader you should have the conversation with your team where each of them are reminded that they are each strong and unique and welcomed.

SELF EXAMINATIONS

1. Mention ways when you have felt unworthy of something?

_____

_____

_____

_____

_____

2. What way do you encourage our team to be whole hearted even at work?

_____

_____

_____

_____

_____

3. What organizational culture does your company take?

_____

_____

_____

_____

_____

4. What is your opinion on your staff's emotional state?

_____

_____

_____

_____

5. What is your organization's stand when it relates to perfectionism and keeping emotions at bay while at work?

_____

_____

_____

_____

_____

6. How can vulnerability be related to being creative, trust worthy and innovative?

_____

_____

_____

_____

_____

7. How have your emotions guided you to make decisions in your workplace?

_____

_____

_____

_____

_____

_____

8. How does your ego play a role in your life?

_____

_____

_____

_____

_____

9. What does perfection mean to you?

_____

_____

_____

_____

_____

10. How do you feel when you hit a milestone or achieve success with your team?

_____

_____

_____

_____

_____

11. What are your coping mechanisms when you are going through suffering and pain at work?

_____

_____

_____

_____

_____

12. What is the intention behind the usage of numbing techniques?

_____

_____

_____

_____

_____

13.Write down situations where you are
   always right or all knowing with your
   team?

_____

_____

_____

_____

_____

14.What method do you encourage in your
   team, hustling for their worth or knowing
   their values?

_____

_____

_____

_____

_____

_____

15. How do you treat people in your organization?

_____

_____

_____

_____

_____

CHECKLISTS

1. Do you possess whole heartedness?

    Yes [　]   No [　]

Does your organization allow its staff to be wholehearted at work?

    Yes [　]   No [　]

2. Do you think your staff should be less emotional when at work?

    Yes [　]   No [　]

3. Do you see vulnerability as a liability in the work place?

    Yes [　]   No [　]

4. Do you encourage your staff to re-learn and stay curious?

Yes [ ]   No [ ]

5. Is there a correlation between our emotions and creativity/innovation?

Yes [ ]   No [ ]

6. Do you lock up your emotions in order not to make decisions based on what you feel?

Yes [ ]   No [ ]

7. Do you believe that we most times make decisions based on our emotions even without our consent?

Yes [ ]   No [ ]

8. Do you protect your ego so as to not feel shame?

Yes [ ]   No [ ]

9. Does your organization drive perfectionist and foster of failure?

Yes [　]　　No [　]

10.　　Do you practice gratitude and celebrate little victories as a team?

Yes [　]　　No [　]

11. Do you pick up numb measures to tackle pain and suffering?

Yes [　]　　No [　]

12.Are you always right and all knowing?

Yes [　]　　No [　]

13.Do you lead for compliance and control?

Yes [　]　　No [　]

14.Are you an armored leader or a daring leader?

Yes [　]　　No [　]

SECTION FOUR: SHAME AND EMPATHY

Here the author talks about shame, the resistance, and confrontation of shame. We have all felt shame at some point, it is almost impossible not to feel shame at all because as long as we care about being normal and like everyone else the fear of being different will always be with us, and shame will always cause pain. Shame resistance can be taught and everyone should learn it.

Shame resistance is when a person can be brave and courageous in the moment of shame to continue without being made a fool of and to emerge with more courage and experience than we had going into it. Shame resilience is the process of moving from shame to empathy by being empathetic. You don't necessarily need to have gone through an experience; having gone through emotions associated with the experience besides, empathy is a choice and a vulnerable one at that because if you choose to connect with someone you would have to connect to the part of you that has experienced that same emotion.

While we talk to people and see them in their most vulnerable, it's in our nature to want to make the situation better but empathy is not about finding the light at the end of the tunnel, it is about walking in the darkness with the person.

KEY TAKEAWAYS

1. The major reason why people avoid vulnerability is how terrifying taking off the armor is, how exposed we are to shame.

2. Shame is the emotion that tells us that we are never good enough but its power to make us feel we are not worthy is unmatched in the realm of emotion.

3. Shame is universal and primitive; the only people that don't experience shame are those who lack the capacity for human condition.

4. People often mistake shame with humiliation, guilt and embarrassment but there are all different things. Shame is not the cure it is the cause.

5. Shame is in no way an indicator of moral behavior rather it drives hurtful immoral and destructive behavior.

6. When looking to shame within your team, it is important to look for perfectionism,

gossiping, harassment, discrimination, cover ups, etc.

7. The most common tool used to show shame is always comparison and it also stifles the innovation and creativity. Comparison should never be used as a management tool.

8. In leadership, you would always be faced with tough decisions like firing someone. It is important to hold the dignity of the person at heart and be kind.

9. There is no possible way to resist shame as long as we care about connection shame resilience is the ability to practice authenticity when we experience shame and go through the experience without sacrificing our values.

10. Self comparison is the ability to be gentle with ourselves when we are faced with shame.

11. When someone is in pain or in a bad situation we tend to try to placate them by downplaying the situation, it is very unwise.

Tell it as it is and let the person deal with the pain.

12. In bad situations it is not our job to try to connect and take the perspective of someone else.

13. To be empathetic means to see the work as others see it to be non-judgmental, to be judgmental, to understand. To understand people's feelings and to communicate your understanding of those feelings.

14. One of the major reasons people shy away from showing emotions is because there is a lot going underneath so they just go for the simplest emotions like fear and anger.

15. Empathy simply means that we are united commonly by our discomfort rather than just pushing and it's just the world view.

SELF EXAMINTIONS

1. What would be your reason for not embracing vulnerability?

_____

_____

_____

_____

_____

2. How does the fear of shame affect you and your zeal to be vulnerable?

_____

_____

_____

_____

_____

3. What are your unwanted identities?

_____

_____

_____

_____

_____

4. How do you handle shame?

_____

_____

_____

_____

_____

5. How has shame acted as a compass for moral behavior for you?

_____

_____

_____

_____

_____

6. What do you consider as the difference between guilt and shame?

_____

_____

_____

_____

_____

7. How can you spot shame within your team members?

_____

_____

_____

_____

_____

8. What are the indicators of shame you can point out?

_____

_____

_____

_____

_____

9. What kind of management tool do you use when trying to boost creativity and innovation?

_____

_____

_____

_____

10. How do you make tough decisions like letting go of someone?

_____

_____

_____

_____

_____

11. What methods have you use to try to resist shame and did it prove to be effective?

_____

_____

_____

_____

_____

12. How do you practice self compassion?

_____

_____

_____

_____

13. What does empathy mean to you?

_____

_____

_____

_____

_____

14. How do you handle the situation when a team member is going through a rough patch as a leader?

_____

_____

_____

_____

15. What are the empathy skills you can imbibe when dealing with your team?

_____

_____

_____

_____

CHECKLISTS

1. Does vulnerability bring shame?

   Yes [ ]   No [ ]

2. Do you possess unwanted identities that you absolutely do not want to be associated with?

   Yes [ ]   No [ ]

3. Does everybody feel shame?

   Yes [ ]   No [ ]

4. Does fear and shame drive unethical behavior?

   Yes [ ]   No [ ]

5. Can shame and empathy co-exist?

   Yes [ ]   No [ ]

6. Is shame and guilt the same thing?

   Yes [ ]   No [ ]

7. Can you spot shame in your organization?

   Yes [ ]   No [ ]

8. Should compassion of staff be used as a management tools to boost creativity and innovation?

   Yes [ ]   No [ ]

9. Do you handle firing a person with the dignity of the person at heart?

   Yes [ ]   No [ ]

10. Are your team members free to talk about shame?

    Yes [ ]   No [ ]

11. Can self-compassion heal you of shame?

    Yes [ ]   No [ ]

12. Have you ever felt empathy for your team member?

        Yes [   ]   No [   ]

13. Are you willing to see the world from others perspective?

        Yes [   ]   No [   ]

14. Do you value the feelings and views of others on a particular matter?

        Yes [   ]   No [   ]

15. Do you think shame, anger and fear Is related to honesty especially when you are communicating it to others?

        Yes [   ]   No [   ]

SECTION FIVE: CURIOSITY AND GROUNDED CONFIDENCE

In this section the author talks about how major confidence is the way of knowing and unknowing, trying and failing and recovering from a few misses.

This type of confidence is not arrogant or fake; it's serious real and based on self-awareness and practice. We cannot believe that we can let our guard down and go through our daily life without fear most of us build our emotional walls early in our lives probably because at a younger age we needed to. Many times the emotional walls made it almost impossible for us to be hurt or let down, feeling left out or unloved sometimes we have had to use the emotional walls to trauma. When we are familiar with unsafe environments where there is violence, racism, poverty, sexism, etc. vulnerability can be life-threatening and emotional walls are safe.

Vulnerability has been the main topic all through because it is the most important skill of courage-building when we develop the confidence to deal with vulnerability and discomfort rather than armoring up, running away or shutting down prepares us for life, building trust, learning to rise etc.

The author also talks about practicing vulnerability and how one way to show your motives is to share your experiences. And practice self-awareness if we lack self-awareness as leaders and when we're disconnected with the intentions driving our thoughts, feelings, and action we won't be able to see bigger pictures.

KEY TAKEAWAYS

1. Grounded confidence is the process of learning and unlearning, and surviving a few misses. It is not founded on arrogance, but rather on self-awareness and practice.

2. Funny enough when leaders realize courage transforms the way we lead we immediately pick up grounded confidence.

3. Vulnerability is the greatest casualty of trauma especially when you find yourself in unsafe environments confronted with many social vices. This is the reason why people find armoring safe and vulnerability life threatening.

4. When leaders have grounded courage, they most likely preach courage, praise effort and

model grit instead of trying to fix others and praise only when results are seen.

5. Vulnerability as a fundamental skill of courage building prepares us for living into our values, building trust and learning to rise.

6. Grounded confidence helps us to rely on the skills we have developed and allows us to focus on higher order challenges.

7. Having the skills to hold tension and discomfort allows us to give care to others and leaders who cannot lean towards vulnerability are often unable to hold the tension of the complexities that are inherited in entrepreneurship.

8. Truthfully building vulnerability and rumbling skills is not easy because easy learning does not build strong skills. Easy learning does not actually instill lasting learning.

9. Practicing vulnerability is never easy or comfortable but practicing it over time brings

in grounded confidence and it helps us create a space to handle it.

10. Simply put, grounded confidence is actually putting together rumbling skills, curiosity and constant practice.

11. Leading effectively means respecting and never aging the different views of your staff and staying curious about the possibility of conflict.

12. We should some level of knowledge or awareness before we can get curious; it is not possible to be curious about something we are unaware of.

13. When productivity is low amongst your team it is often attributed to the organizational culture at that time. It is important to look inward and fix that culture first.

14. As a leader, focus on asking questions. Experiment with your staff, encourage vulnerability and drive continuous improvement ultimately.

15. Engaging in a daring leadership ultimately means to practice vulnerability, become self aware and to engage in tough conversations. Also be intentional about building trust and commit to helping those and commit to helping those who are normally silenced.

SELF EXAMINATIONS

1. What kind of confidence do you possess?

_____

_____

_____

_____

_____

2. In what way have you built armor around yourself to protect you from hurt or disappointment?

_____

_____

_____

_____

3. What is the cause of your armored life?

_____

_____

_____

_____

4. How do you prepare your team for success?

_____

_____

_____

_____

5. How can vulnerability be used to build courage and confidence members?

_____

_____

_____

_____

6. In what way has constant practice and experience helped you out of a difficult situation with your team?

_____

_____

_____

_____

_____

7. As a leader, how do you handle the tension of paradoxes that accompany the job?

_____

_____

_____

_____

_____

8. How does your leadership thrive in the face of opposites?

_____

_____

_____

_____

9. How easy do you make learning for your team members?

_____

_____

_____

_____

_____

10. What does it mean to lead effectively?

_____

_____

_____

_____

_____

11. Can you explain how curiosity affects leadership?

_____

_____

_____

_____

12. What organizational culture exists in your organization or with your team?

_____

_____

_____

_____

_____

13. How important are the human resources in your organization and are they involved in making decisions for the company?

_____

_____

_____

_____

_____

14. What would make up the components of a daring leadership?

_____

_____

_____

_____

_____

15. How would you tackle problems of the organization or team especially when it threatens the mission, values and vision?

_____

_____

_____

_____

_____

CHECKLISTS

1. Do you have confidence in yourself?

   Yes [ ]   No [ ]

2. Is your confidence fostered on the fact that you practice regularly and that you are self-aware?

   Yes [ ]   No [ ]

3. Do you take up self-protection to stay physically and emotionally safe?

   Yes [ ]   No [ ]

4. Do you praise your team members only when there are visible results?

Yes [　]　　No [　]

5. Do you agree that vulnerability is the fundamental skill of courage building?

Yes [　]　　No [　]

6. Is it important to build experience through practice?

Yes [　]　　No [　]

7. Are tensions and discomfort an important skill for leaders to learn?

Yes [　]　　No [　]

8. Are you okay with the way you land the ambiguity of paradoxes in your organization?

Yes [　]　　No [　]

9. Do you believe that learning should be an easy task?

Yes [　]　　No [　]

10. Do you lead your team members effectively?

Yes [ ]   No [ ]

11. Are you a curious leader?

Yes [ ]   No [ ]

12. Is there a link between being curious and gaining grounded confidence?

Yes [ ]   No [ ]

13. Do you empower your team to take vulnerability and turn it into strength?

Yes [ ]   No [ ]

14. Do you consider yourself a daring leader?

Yes [ ]   No [ ]

15. Do you believe that people are the most important part of your work?

Yes [ ]   No [ ]

PART TWO: LIVING INTO OUR VALUES

In this part the author talks about daring leaders who live into their values and are never silent about their hard times especially during trying times when we are trying to behave like everything is okay. Everything can be confusing and overpowering in the moments when we start thinking about irrelevant people and what negative things they had told us, we start to forget what made us go into the arena in the first place the reason we're there and the reason we have gone this far.

Most times the things we believe in are what allow us to start projects; we are going to try doing something we would not normally do because we believe we have values.

One thing about values is that while courage requires us to let down our guard when we are about to do something, we don't have to enter situations that are difficult or though unprepared.

This part also talks about a big question, "What boundaries do I need to put in place for me to be in my integrity and generous with my assumptions about the intentions, words, and actions of others?"

The behaviors and skills that support seemingly simple beliefs are not as complicated as those that support the assumptions of positive intent, but they are most times, more complicated than what we might have expected.

KEY TAKEAWAYS

1. When we are faced with tough and dark moments and we are trying to be brave, we may be pushed into confusion, distractions and noise and we will be looking for ways out, it is easy to forget our values, try not to.

2. Our values are what lead into those difficult and uncomfortable situations and when we stumble in there, our values should remind us why we want it.

3. Clarity of value is an essential support to a daring leader when coupled with rumble skills and tools.

4. Living our values means to define those values, narrowing them into at least two core values that are deeply crystallized into our minds and that are clear, unassailable, precise and do not ever feel like a choice.

5. Living our values also mean to not stop at just talking about it but also to practice it into the very fiber of our behavior even at great moments of discomfort.

6. Empathy and self-compassion are also very important aspects of living our values. It is good to continue having those difficult conversations, push against secrecy and judgment between our team.

7. A brave leader is not someone who has all the answers or who can facilitate a flawless discussion. It is someone who sees and hears and listens and asks questions and is willing to continue to be in that uncomfortable situation.

8. Self compassion reminds us that if we cannot cheer ourselves on, then we should not expect others to do it.

9. Having someone who knows your values and supports your efforts to live in them, this person(s) can help to show you empathy when it gets too hard.

10. As daring leaders, giving feedback and getting good at receiving feedback are necessary skills.

11. Receiving feedback involves listening, integrating feedback and reflecting it back with accountability. It simply means to hold the discomfort it brings you and divert it into great energy.

12. Letting your team know your values and knowing theirs allows both parties to actually get to know each other and work better.

13. When people are taught how to give and receive daring feedback, a circle of trust, positive intention and self-awareness is built amongst the team.

14. Knowing the values of people you to know them and what they stand for.

15. In leadership, there will always be times of darkness but if we are clear about the values we set, it will serve as the light to put us out of that situation.

SELF EXAMINATIONS

1. In times of great despair and daring moments what emotions do you feel?

_____

_____

_____

_____

_____

2. When faced with great despair, what do you choose to do?

_____

_____

_____

_____

_____

3. What are your values as a leader?

_____

_____

_____

_____

_____

4. Mention a situation where values put you in an uncomfortable situation?

_____

_____

_____

_____

_____

5. What do you understand as living your values?

_____

_____

_____

_____

_____

6. Write down two core values you have?

_____

_____

_____

_____

_____

7. In what way are you practicing and applying these values to your everyday behavior?

_____

_____

_____

_____

8. What would hinder you from applying your values into your behavior?

_____

_____

_____

_____

_____

9. How can you in-cooperate self compassion and empathy into living your values?

_____

_____

_____

_____

_____

10. How do you handle getting feedback especially when it is not what you hoped?

_____

_____

_____

_____

_____

11. How does courage and bravery come into play when you are dealing with handling feedback?

_____

_____

_____

_____

_____

12. What is an example of a meaningful feedback?

_____

_____

_____

_____

_____

13. How can your values help you out of a dark moment as a leader?

_____

_____

_____

_____

_____

14. How do you live self-compassion?

_____

_____

_____

_____

_____

15. What is the process of giving feedback?

_____

_____

_____

_____

_____

CHECKLISTS

1. When faced with great despair, do you look for an easy way out that promises relief?

    Yes [   ]   No [   ]

2. Have your values ever put you in an uncomfortable and difficult situation?

    Yes [   ]   No [   ]

3. Have your values ever helped you through an uncomfortable and difficult situation?

    Yes [   ]   No [   ]

4. Do you have clarity of values?

    Yes [   ]   No [   ]

5. Do you just profess values but do not actually live them?

    Yes [   ]   No [   ]

6. Are your values properly defined?

    Yes [   ]   No [   ]

7. Can you self-identify with your values?

    Yes [ ]   No [ ]

8. Are your values evident in your everyday behavior?

    Yes [ ]   No [ ]

9. Do you have the ability to foster empathy?

    Yes [ ]   No [ ]

10. Is self-compassion necessary?

    Yes [ ]   No [ ]

11. Are you brave enough to get feedback without having backlash?

    Yes [ ]   No [ ]

12. Do you know the values of your team members?

    Yes [ ]   No [ ]

13. Is leadership always a joyful ride?

Yes [ ]   No [ ]

14. Are values a reflection of who people actually is?

Yes [ ]   No [ ]

15. Can your values help you out of a difficult situation?

Yes [ ]   No [ ]

PART THREE: BRAVING TRUST

In this part the author talks about being brave and putting it into practice. She also talks about how to emotionally defend ourselves and bring up all our defenses because we want to be trustworthy and we want people to believe we are trustworthy. So when people start showing signs of distrust we go into freak out mode even though funny enough we struggle and find it very hard to trust others. Many people want to believe that they are trustworthy but do not see others as that. Believing we are trustworthy and others believing we are trustworthy are two different things.

According to Charles Feltman's definitions of trust and distrust, trust is defined as choosing to risk making something you value vulnerable to another person's actions and distrust is deciding that what is important to you is not safe with this person in this situation or any situation at all. By these definitions we can understand why we can become hostile when we talk about trust, how would we feel if someone told us they do not feel we could be trusted in any situation at all.

The author also talks about how trust is rough and how the conversations about trust can go sideways fast. We often avoid trouble, and that does not make things better.

Trust is perceived to be the glue that holds teams and organizations together. If we don't want to enhance our performances and the performances of our teams or organizations then we ignore the trust issues that we have. The only way to ensure full effectiveness in our workplace or anywhere else is to find possible ways to solve our trust issues.

KEY TAKEAWAYS

1. Trust is a very touchy subject for people and questioning it most times leads to lockdown of our emotions.

2. We all want to believe that we are trustworthy, even though ironically, we struggle to trust others.

3. Trust is choosing to risk making something you value vulnerable to another person's action and distrust is deciding that what is important is not safe with a person in a particular situation.

4. When we struggle with trust and do not have the skills to talk about it with the person involved, we tend to talk about people instead of the one involved.

5. Research shows that trust is the glue that holds teams and organizations together and when ignored, it is at the expense of the team's performance.

6. As leaders we need to have a conversation guide to use with colleagues that would aid with trust building.

7. Confidentiality not only means not sharing what people tell you but it also entails the fact that we do not share other people's experiences.

8. Integrity means choosing courage over comfort, choosing right over what is fun, fast or easy and practicing your values not just professing them.

9. Integrity comes with great difficulty and the perception of a lack of it brings instant wariness within your team.

10. A daring leader would not delegate important work to staff that would not ask for help because they do not have trust that they would not have the ability to stretch their capacity.

11. Elements like boundaries, reliability, accountability, vault-integrity, non-judgment and generosity are ingredients of a trust building conversations.

12. Embracing personal accountability creates courage and also aids in building vulnerability.

13. Teams should work together to develop observable behaviors for the elements of trust earlier discussed.

14. You cannot earn trust by demanding it; trust is earned by the stacking of small moments over time and cannot be summoned with a command.

15. Self trust is the foundation of trust with others. However, it is one of the first things we lose when we fail or experience setbacks. The braving theory also applies to us.

85

SELF EXAMINATIONS

1. Why do you think you are trustworthy?

_____

_____

_____

_____

_____

2. Mention instances when you have trusted other people?

_____

_____

_____

_____

3. What could make you distrust a person?

_____

_____

_____

_____

_____

4. How do you handle a situation where you don't trust your colleague?

_____

_____

_____

_____

_____

5. What are the skills needed to tackle trust issues?

_____

_____

_____

_____

_____

6. What is the link between trust and connectivity within your team?

_____

_____

_____

_____

_____

7. To what extent is trust evident in your organization?

_____

_____

_____

_____

_____

8. What rumble tool would you use with colleagues helps us in conversations of curiosity, learning and ultimately trust building?

_____

_____

_____

_____

_____

9. What roles does confidentiality play in your team?

_____

_____

_____

_____

_____

10. How do you practice integrity in your organization?

_____

_____

_____

_____

_____

11. What leads you to judge people?

_____

_____

_____

_____

_____

12. As daring leaders, how important is your need for team members to ask questions?

_____

_____

_____

_____

_____

13. How can you practice personal accountability and foster courage?

_____

_____

_____

_____

_____

14. What are the methods in which someone can earn your trust?

_____

_____

_____

_____

_____

15. What is the basis for trusting yourself especially when you face setbacks?

_____

_____

_____

_____

_____

CHECKLISTS

1. Are you a trustworthy person?

    Yes [   ]   No [   ]

2. Do you trust people especially your colleagues?

    Yes [   ]   No [   ]

3. Have you had a bad situation where you are distrustful of someone?

    Yes [   ]   No [   ]

4. Can you communicate trust with the person who is involved?

    Yes [   ]   No [   ]

5. Can distrust amongst your team bring about disconnection?

    Yes [   ]   No [   ]

6. Is trust a must have in your organization?

    Yes [   ]   No [   ]

7. Have you ever had a conversation about trust building with your colleagues?

    Yes [   ]   No [   ]

8. Do you consider confidentiality as important to trust building?

    Yes [   ]   No [   ]

9. Do you practice and encourage integrity?

    Yes [   ]   No [   ]

10. Do you practice no judgment in your team?

    Yes [   ]   No [   ]

11. Does asking for help make you seem weak?

    Yes [   ]   No [   ]

12. Do you agree that personal accountability is important?

    Yes [   ]   No [   ]

13. Can trust be easily earned?

Yes [ ]   No [ ]

14. Is self trust important to your personal growth?

Yes [ ]   No [ ]

15. Do you trust yourself?

Yes [ ]   No [ ]

PART FOUR: LEARNING TO RISE

Here, the author talks about preparing for tough times and hard landings, and how leaders should try their best to teach how to deal with disappointment or setbacks before it occurs not after or during.

Due to research, leaders who have been trained in rising skills as a part of courage-building programs are most likely to take risks and engage in courageous behaviors. If they fail or fall, they can recover. Not having the skills mentioned above won't help braver leadership. And also teaching or helping people how to recover or get back on their feet after they have failed or fallen is more difficult.

This is why we try to teach people and make them ready to deal with failure or falling upfront.

KEY TAKEAWAYS

1. Leaders who are going through daring leadership should prepare for hard landings. When you are brave and willing to risk failure, you should expect hard landings.

2. Teach skills for rising or resilience before going into a project so that the team members would be equipped with the knowledge of how to handle problems as they come and also know how to get back up after being knocked down.

3. Failing and falling strongly relates with shame and that is where the skills of vulnerability come into place.

4. Millennial have a harder time accepting a daring leader because they are so accustomed to engaging with technology and avoiding face to face conversations on failure, shame, and vulnerability.

5. The learning to rise process is about getting up from our failures, overcoming our mistakes and facing hurt in a way that brings more wisdom into our lives.

6. We are emotional beings and when something hard happens to us, thinking and behavior are driven by our emotions.

7. Very few people are emotionally curious about situations they are in but when you

do, you are removed from the feeling of discomfort and frustration.

8. While others would automatically take up the person or situation that hurt their emotions, risers would get curious about what is going on and figure out why and what they are feeling.

9. People often offload emotions and ill feelings unto others because it is easier than feeling it by ourselves.

10. Living, working and growing on eggshells creates huge cracks in our sense of safety and self-worth.

11. When we stockpile hurt throughout our lives, it always affects us by shutting down our systems and forcing us to face the problems. This usually happens as mid life crisis.

12. People who have too many cheery claims and do not struggle with bad tones are often just putting a camouflage of what is actually going on beneath the surface.

13. A major strategy for reckoning with emotions instead of offloading it is actually just inhaling deeply and exhaling.

14. Anxiety is one of the most contagious emotions. That's why one person's anxiety can send the whole team into a tailspin. As contagious as anxiety is, so also is calm, so a daring leader must learn how to dispel anxiety and accept calm.

15. Success should be a reflection of who you are, what you want and what brings joy. Success should never be defined by anyone else than yourself.

SELF EXAMINATIONS

1. What are the rising and resilience skills your team members need to be equipped with?

_____

_____

_____

_____

2. In your organization, how do you encourage productivity, is it through striving for perfection or encouraging failing and falling?

_____

_____

_____

_____

_____

_____

3. Give an example of when you faced setbacks and the action you took after that?

_____

_____

_____

_____

_____

_____

4. How can you come out of an emotional mess?

_____

_____

_____

_____

_____

5. What are the questions you ask yourself when you are in a bad place that suggest emotional curiosity?

_____

_____

_____

_____

_____

6. How do you recognize that you have a problem with your emotions?

_____

_____

_____

_____

7. Have you accumulated hurt so much and what outcome did you get?

_____

_____

_____

_____

_____

8. Can you describe how you experience pain and hurtful moments?

_____

_____

_____

_____

_____

9. At what point in your life do you experience symptoms of stock piling emotions in your life?

_____

_____

_____

_____

_____

10. What are the emotions you stockpile so you
    don't feel?

_____

_____

_____

_____

_____

11. Mention the emotions you use to hide the
    emotions you feel?

_____

_____

_____

_____

_____

12. Give an example of when your anxiety as a leader affected your team?

_____

_____

_____

_____

_____

13. What is your definition of success?

_____

_____

_____

_____

_____

14. How can you handle braving and fear altogether?

_____

_____

_____

_____

CHECKLISTS

1. Are your team members equipped with rising skills?

       Yes [   ]   No [   ]

2. Do you encourage failing or falling in your organizations?

       Yes [   ]   No [   ]

3. Are your emotions the drivers of your behavior?

       Yes [   ]   No [   ]

4. Can you recognize when your emotions are affecting your behaviors and stop it?

       Yes [   ]   No [   ]

5. Are you emotionally curious?

       Yes [   ]   No [   ]

6. Do you often off load your emotion unto others?

Yes [ ]   No [ ]

7. Have you had an unexpected outburst due to accumulated hurt over time?

Yes [ ]   No [ ]

8. Do people constantly walk on eggshell around you?

Yes [ ]   No [ ]

9. Is it easier to acknowledge hurt than to get angry and pissed off?

Yes [ ]   No [ ]

10. Do you often pile up emotions of hurt so that you do not feel them?

Yes [ ]   No [ ]

11. Are you an anxious leader?

Yes [ ]   No [ ]

12. Can your anxiety positively affect your team members?

    Yes [ ]   No [ ]

13. Do you feel insecure as a leader?

    Yes [ ]   No [ ]

14. Is your success defined by someone else?

    Yes [ ]   No [ ]

15. Are you willing to choose the adventure of being brave and afraid at the same time?

    Yes [ ]   No [ ]

CPSIA information can be obtained
at www.ICGtesting.com
Printed in the USA
LVHW111601141220
674149LV00031B/920